D1446632

Sleepers Awake

Sleepers Awake

POEMS

Oli Hazzard

FARRAR, STRAUS AND GIROUX

NEW YORK

Farrar, Straus and Giroux
120 Broadway, New York 10271

Originally published in 2024 by Carcanet, Great Britain
Published in the United States by Farrar, Straus and Giroux
First American edition, 2025

Library of Congress Cataloging-in-Publication Data
Names: Hazzard, Oli, 1986– author.
Title: Sleepers awake : poems / Oli Hazzard.
Description: First American edition. | New York : Farrar, Straus and Giroux,
    2025.
Identifiers: LCCN 2024034058 | ISBN 9780374616182 (paperback)
Subjects: LCGFT: Poetry.
Classification: LCC PR6108.A99 S54 2025 | DDC 811/.54—
    dc23/eng/20240726
LC record available at https://lccn.loc.gov/2024034058

Designed by Andrew Latimer

Our books may be purchased in bulk for promotional, educational, or
business use. Please contact your local bookseller or the Macmillan Corporate
and Premium Sales Department at 1-800-221-7945, extension 5442,
or by email at MacmillanSpecialMarkets@macmillan.com.

www.fsgbooks.com
Follow us on social media at @fsgbooks

10 9 8 7 6 5 4 3 2 1

for Ned and Frank and Tess

CONTENTS

Sleepers Awake

PROGRESS: REAL AND IMAGINED

Why, stand under and understand is all one.
The Two Gentlemen of Verona

For a long time
I wondered
what's all this juice for?

to bring us closer?

to touch or meet
you here

in this
small downed
"room"

take
the sensation

of eyes
moving
as a totem

alive and googling
the anonymous green blossom

humming in the air
out of frame.

O, Johannes
there you are

a little word
for the prose

are we to piece
together a spillage

on the
"still page"

so
an ache
still may take

place
in public?

§

location, plate

    just
happy to live
      from work
in the "milky
      circle"

the light is matte
on my hand
on my crook

My clap is
how many

motets
nuanced

by
the gross
interiors of

freshly transparent
minsters

to bump eyes
          on, take
dictation
          from

the lordliest
pace of

field activity
from which

senile
snailshell

an irritating
if melismatic
churning noise
emerges

§

Go back a bit

to hover-read

the sharpened block

for rain to be "tomentose".

The day is itchy
with desire not

to show how much
I wants to show

it said to myself,
hoping to be
overthrow

"Morning plaza"
wet grass

glass
recycling
overflow.

I seemed to wander
in a specious field,

the canal as clear
as +1,

the bus late.

The medieval poet remains
a leisure deity

bizarre, I accept.

I fancied
"Britishness"

evenly
distributed

among arrow keys

space bar

drizzling lightly
inside

a pause in
applause.

Reading Peppa Pig
upside down

difficulty bludgeons
me as memorable

my own performance
of exhaustion

memorable.
News of

knives
and forks

neuter of contrafactus

I remember the shadow
of the bank headquarters
as an enormous
see-through parfait

5pm "unfolding"

a moot song

§

mute the time
and something in
creases inside me

unfolds
a clear aesthetic goal:

secure what
the historical pet
felt like

here we are
at capacity

the slump between
clarity and
unhappiness

trivial reprieve

if you're happy
and you know it

is it worth it

son
plugged into
song

"Nothing more real
Than boredom—"   *Oppen*

a feeling
of ob
long:

dreamlessness
lessness
ness

§

gardener father
teacher mother

shapes of
non-human
exactness

put this down
pick this up

a fresh

I can barely put
the dishes away

kind of aesthetic

tiny brown, black,
white and beige dots
the nail of my index finger

an injury pitched

just below the threshold

of interest

voice breaking
in ten-minute previews

my own sexual "style"
is to encourage
and complain
at the same time

a flickering, momentary
hallucination

I have no idea why
light changes

pavement
swallows

last leaf bits
capsize in

eczemary air
nothing is so beautiful

as when you say
ok, reluctantly

you can tell me
your funded dream

about daylight

§

Thursday's
daily buffering
of quondam form

beleagurable sense

last night
one or the other

stirred, coughed, or wept
in his sleep
this morning

the ample shadow
of the maple
gums the pavement

staring at people
longingly or sadly

from a distance
of eight inches

an almost
physically painful task

like suddenly yourself
brushed you

and shushed

still waiting
for something
to cling

to the latticework
of the feeling

§

Blue light

Green leaf

A whole useless

Sensory life

IP: 31.81.239.234
Timestamp: 2020-06-04 11:
11:30 UTC

For a long time
exhaustion

and its ostentatious display
were a big part

of the work. For a long time

§

the labour
was thinking about

the fictional workplace

the "thinking"
doesn't happen in

True, by that point
the object is
swallowed by language

though by that point
language has itself
become an object, so

There is a way
to be exact
and at the same time stupid

A commonplace

Where I am

Strange like the
ballooning

nimbus

Where you have
just a few memories

A special rejection

of the recently discovered
Ears of Earth

Where
Is it worth it

here I appear to pause

§

Here in pose
a pear appears

I put that in
to make it
more hummy

is it worth it

the daily catastrophe
of the camouflage
bigger than the head

what is being done and
only just in plain sight

an historic address
in anachronistic dress

True, childhood
was a weak creation

Avoiding work, however

Book 1 previews
in late August.

Fold the pages, cut them
and stuff into the mouth and eyes.

Thus

accidents and poetry
descend directly from the sky

fluting my phone
yodelling in the bean-flower

Trying to remember
the basics

Trying to remember

"spring is
a bourgeois
climate"

Boris
fucking
Becker

§

Once again
only one form:

theft, or
dramatization

of a dogmatic theory

or
wait

for light

to detail
Tuesday air.

Ah ok. So it's
February

picket
donut

and death is
"a medium of exemplary blandness"

which represents an opportunity
for "new forms of expressiveness"

so said the designated driver.

So I said
something so familiar like

with staying up
to date

am I even able
to close my eyes??

But someone looked at me
today through the window
and my insides capsized

O Johannes

reflect

on that. White glove

flouting the form

20

twatting a thrush
straight out the sky

poetry without any ideas in it

brimming with a real stupidity

Little dots of brownish white
flicked against the pane and dried.

Paddled
Mottled

Lake—sweet

§

Extracting the ore
from boredom . . .

Listening to the language
talking to itself

To alter what it says
I write myself to sleep

Where I am moved slightly
by analogue

Music, by analogy
with scratches, striations

In the four
seasons, the only music

I've ever heard . . .

It's like there was actually no information
to be had

except what you doodle
while on the landline.

What kind of child
was anyone?

I don't really hear him
except when

I confuse
with myself

you. Does it really
feel like this

where we are
nose to nose

in an aluminium

drum. A transparent sphere
living coloured

in. Feels tight
in the aluminium drum

of the memory
of the things I liked.

"Confusion is painful—
spacious." What if

every time you laughed
you were sick . . . ?

I was writing this in bed
the children thrown to sleep   *Mayer*

and thought I heard rain
and then out the window

though it took a while
the trees started to nod.

For a long time
I was trying to visualise
a long and tangled root system

a signature in the soil
when you asked

if I was listening.

Days pass . . .

It has something to do
with this

this glitch
upon which

this has come
to depend

§

Sorry . . . when I try to strike a deal
My children, who don't accept the premise of work
Hallucinate themselves out of earshot

At the picket, the standing around
"A native time"

Unconvinced, C, D, and E receive a bunch of anxious emails
As though some conviction could crystallise
From the intersection of external convictions
A vector of sweetness
Vital, trivial

Gold is formed during the death of a star.

There you are.

One poem, but inside it
hundreds of smaller poems

each with an agenda of its own

pupae in the rotten bark

we pick off "Minty", a stump

that kills an hour

ten weeks

into an indeterminate period

my phone has been hacked

I google, in the hope

it might spook the hacker

It's not that I *want*

to be surveilled, exactly

but—those emails—*you might be interested in?*—

It's hard not to be touched

when someone really listens, ha ha!

Back to office
expression on my face

Knowing you're being duped

Kind of enjoying it

Watching the image of the plane you're on

Humming during sex

Shaving while eating

Writing while hoovering

Cursing seagulls

What's worse

Exposure or occlusion

Imperfect synonyms

Imperfect antonyms

Something so complicated you'll never be able to
understand even the basic terms involved

Something so simple you understood it a long
time ago, without even noticing

"Days" pass . . .

I wondered

Is it worth
even breathing in

Spring's smithereens

empty snailshell
worm stub retreat

green glass sharkfin
beard hair, split in 3

is it worth
to feel something
            to a present not

at extent

lucky to

live from

work

in

the "milky

circle"

§

Dear Oli
            How pleased
                        I am to get
your letter
            sad as it is. Oli Oli
                        Oli what shall
I say. What did
            you want to be
                        when you were a boy?
Ho Ho what man
            are you this morning
                        as you read this
and the labyrinth
            of your day
                        complexes itself
before you?
            Are you picking
                        your nose or
playing chess or
            scratching your head?????
                        Write and give
me some idea
            of the texture of
                        your happiness

at this moment
    My texts are green
       so

that I may experience high
levels of interest in
Louis the Pious, in the Diocese
I felt my interest
returning, and yet
Pater describes the transportation
of soils from different regions
To Richmond International Airport
As a mixture of tiny brown,
black, white and beige dots
Somehow expressed by the level
of his waistband
Which looks like a data centre
and in fact must be, since
More obvious ruptures
in period detail
Don't upset or disturb
they comfort, in fact
Since they ruin the experience of
And so on
Over there by
the fence is another bird
I don't know how to name.
This is a little thing
we have done together.
We have a go at the grammar
the lines refuse to sequence

around and
    want them all

for the fruits they harbour.
  Limited
to want everything

rain
pip-divoting
a pivoting breeze

In bright and open space

doodling in the centre
of my life

I found myself loving
some more than others
which gave me hope
that I, too, might be

wrong, I was wrong, I
clapped and clapped

fumbling the orchestration

crackling water in the ear

here I appear to await . . .   *(from G—)*

which is when I thought
of my friends—*most bitterly*, Johannes!

their proper names, floating around
like tiny cursors on my retina
provoking me into an act of refocussing

the way for example touching someone's skin
and feeling very far away, not just from them
but from your own hand, which recedes
as though backing away
from an embarrassing mistake
it could still get away with
can exhaust me enough
to never want to do it again

true sometimes I will simply list basic queries
about the nature of my personality
in order to allow for the possibility that it exists
will I ever not be tired, will I ever not be selfish
will I give over any of my ample domestic space
to a simple description
of the face of one friend, the eruption of exactitude
when her head turns, you know how it goes
when you think about a name
and a part of you cringes, or squeezes itself
inside you, as though lightly injuring you
into an awareness that you're not yet entirely done
with childish feelings, with an appetite
to let the discrepant tones, little dots of colour
distribute themselves among you, and
to just lie yourself down to dry in the sun

the names, Johannes
you were thinking about the names

for untrained hands

how best to pervert
them, so that they may
be enjoyed by all, uncomplicatedly

and forever

we thought, then, too

about writing a haiku

about standing
in a lake—no, I

thought about
a haiku

about

having paddled
in a dappled

lake—"a sweet

mistake" (Traherne)

But a pain in the centre of my back
For a long time
I had forgotten
The cold brought out

(1886)   On the twentyfourthish

Rain
Pipe distribution
A breeze

Bright and open in the open

Extracting the or
from the refrain

I put the "sigh" in Versailles
to verse, or worse
to work, to—

The poet is dead, and yet
The poems remain . . . excellent

Even here, among their friends

the meadows spread out over there
like some kind of drastic condiment

a rhythm of presence
and increasingly annoying presence

a routine
of surprise
belaboured
until all that's left

is pure inflation,

the boing in
ongoingness.

IP: 31.81.239.234
Timestamp: 2020-04-04 11:
11:30 UTC

A poem should be
like that, all like

statement, suspicion
contempt, fatigue

death by listening

§

The fence is another bird

§

A poem should be like that.
A mixture of small brown,
black, white and
beige dots
Somehow revealed
by the layers of your wrist
Which looks like a data centre
and really should be

§

. . . I wondered if anyone had had the idea of designing some (impossible buildings), which, of course, someone has, when I googled the phrase I came across the website of the Catalan, Barcelona-based artist and photographer I, of whom I'd never heard, but who has created, through a combination of photography and 3D digital rendering, a series of hyper-realistic images of buildings which it would be physically impossible to build in our world ("'The techniques I use are often described as "camera matching" or "perspective matching" and several 3D software packages provide functionalities that allow you to perform this,' he explained, but added that he tends to do a lot of the work by hand to 'reach the level of detail needed to achieve high photorealism'"), at least at the moment, with engineering at its current state of development (who knows, perhaps in forty years' time some new material will have been discovered that will allow such structures to exist), buildings like the oddly-titled *Defence*, which consists of a thin, shabby-looking building which rises vertically about five floors, then from which a much larger block juts out horizontally to the left for dozens of "floors" (though presumably "floors" would be "walls" in that horizontal arrangement), a structure which in reality would, of course, be fatally unbalanced, a lesson which I have been trying to impart to D, when we play with his Duplo, and after a usually quite promising beginning to the process of constructing a tower—a few blocks will clump together to form a rough base, and then an erratic-looking vertebrae, constituted of horribly clashing colours, will start developing upwards out of it, and becoming almost immediately unstable—it will collapse unspectacularly, limply toppling, causing him to cry and become confused and frustrated and angry, feelings which I will try to assuage or mollify by explaining that this event can be prevented from occurring again (or can be made to occur much less frequently) by approaching the task of construction in a more considered and systematic fashion, and as I'm trying to explain this I will also be demonstrating physically how this should be done, first creating a solid, wide, square base, and then building a narrower tower on top of that (look, I say, watch) lacing together into a sturdy object those bricks with six nodules or little circles on top so that forces which will shortly test the integrity of the structure (gravity, a child's finger) will have a greater chance of being absorbed or resisted by being distributed among the seams which both connect and divide the individual blocks, though as I explain this to him he refuses to be comforted, if anything my explanation makes him even more distressed and he begins to wail, which I find difficult to deal with because by this point I have become authentically absorbed in the task of assembling the tower, the activity has become wholly detached from the occasion or the need which gave rise to it, much in the way a poet, in an era long before our own entry into the world, would receive a stipend or a commission from a patron, and in agreeing to receive this fee the poet would commit themselves to paying tribute to the patron in some way in the artwork which the fee enabled (by clearing time for the poet to write poems rather than, presumably, just being destitute or having another job, such as barman, cook, scribe, or clerk, or lawyer, and so on, all of which activities would have diminished the amount of time for the poet to spend thinking about poetic things, though of course the activity of working in a field unrelated to poetry might itself prove equally if not more generative of poetry, depending on the sensibility of the poet), usually through a dedication at the front of the work, in which the patron would sometimes be addressed directly and praised lavishly for their beneficence, their accomplishments in the political world, the nobility of their family, their splendid house, and so on, and though many of these dedications or addresses to patrons are formulaic, and rehearse familiar tropes and employ routine image-sets, others, such as those by J, are obviously ironic, using these familiar tropes in such an exaggerated or histrionic manner that it becomes clear that the poet is lampooning the obligation to gratitude and subservience the poet-patron relationship has enforced upon them, though perhaps most interestingly there are occasional examples in which it becomes apparent, some distance into the dedicatory passage, that despite (or maybe because of) the murky or troubling or unstable circumstances of its composition the poet has become authentically absorbed in the activity of composing, so much so that a degree of imaginative detachment from the originating impulse for the work (whether accepted as a necessary part of the economy of poetic composition, or implicitly rejected as a "corruption" or distortion of the artistic process, which presumably should occur as naturally as leaves to the tree) has been achieved, and that this originating context (or the pretence of one) has in fact entirely evaporated, or has become so obscured by the manoeuvrings of the poet's syntax, which have taken the poet so far into the poem (as though into the labyrinth, from which there seems no escape until it has been escaped) that they cannot see how it began and how it will end, though of course this is merely an unverifiable response I have experienced when reading such poems, and in fact I can imagine how the verisimilitude of the depiction of authentic absorption in the artistic act enabled by a financial transaction which is swiftly transcended might itself represent the most fawning of possible tributes (so gracious and enabling is the patron that they themselves have facilitated their own marginalisation in favour of the foregrounding of the artwork, and so on), especially since even in such instances it's at no point entirely clear who is speaking, the poet or the patron (is the former simply a mouthpiece for the latter, or the latter a platform for the former, and so on), or who is looking over whose shoulder or in what unstable compound these two figures or entities speak through one another . . .

I miss that premise

but I'll put the urge to exclaim to one side
for the moment, since

I just read an essay

in verse, or poem as essay, or something

else

that made me

momentarily concerned

that the statement-counterstatement

model evoked in passing above or below

before being turned away from, à la

whoever, is once again merely a form

of evasion, or "dramatisation of a dialectical principle"

so familiar as to remain unrefreshed

by its reiteration in formal terms.

All of this preamble

pleasurable as it has been!

has merely been leading up to the present moment

during which I turn towards

the question of turning away,

which necessitates an awkward amount

of direct eye contact with you.

How long can you look at this cat for . . . ?

aggression being a kind of intimacy, or vice versa

it was considered a failure

for subjects of the portrait to look away

is to fail. Look at me

when I tell off my son
I see his attention spreading, look

rhetorically, shifting
the premise of the question
has begun

Is it even worth pissing my eyes off?

Am I attractive and can I be thrown out?

Well as I was saying
I am just a normal father
of a normal father
born to end my epidemic.
Narrative is not widely appreciated
by me. Why should I be
so embarrassed?

So the desired "ethic"
goes unelaborated

beneath a calendrical
smudge

like fictive traffic
at the window forever

trying to get to me
to touch myself

with myself.
First with disgust

the lattice
ripples, the

lattice ripples
and blurrs

§

Light fastens

Written satisfaction   water to leaves
Is this why?   then goes somewhere

Rhythm is always   no longer visible.
Animated   With this observation

Fearful appearance   "a remote mote of forest
Before the animus   rests". I can think about you

The option is therefore   now. It—the thought of
Therefore   then . . . how to do with this

Even the closest   what it asks
Basic +1

Yes, it was   Then is a mood / changed. No
Poor, well worth it   only now. I could still leave

Thank you   but the desire to leave
Interdisciplinary system   leaves something

Sign in   to be desired. What does
The Allen Fort   this? I can't even

Probably the most up-to-date situation

The billion parts   an odd pattern the sycamores
Per self   throw—basic

                              midcentury

                              perceptions

                              I plainly see

November light
cork under sides
of branches
over a pond.

Leicestershire's a cretic.

Where can I put this fact

of everyone else, Johannes

A little clearing
for this comfort

to discomfort,
a little hollow
for time to take

place.
When my finger's wet

the phone won't
let me in.

The clean light
on childhood sea:
pins and needles.

Endlessly, reluctantly
I waited

for the delivery
of the decent dream

over there
in poetry

where
I wait for me

reluctantly.
Reluctantly

childhood

was my masterpiece

of work avoidance, yet
now it's late, or later, and everything's

cancelled. Late August in   Book 1 Preview
    May, the suspension of   On him.
is to be ahead of it, so that we   Mark is tired of the scheme
    might finish by accident and   Poetry straight out of the sky

OK. I am trying to recall . . .

. . . the name

        this activity was given . . .

. . . doing something
        for the first time . . .

            . . . for the last time . . .

a way of
        being precise
                and inexact at once

a commonplace,
a lordly pleasurehouse

I'm for
        getting together
                awkwardly in—

. . . ossein . . .

. . . the noises
        ingested . . .

                . . . weird, three-eared

melody's lodestar . . .

§

where was I?
        Name
                where I am

awkward   A common dream

    While my kids   Trend:
                              Cell damage

watch Paw Patrol,

like

Just a few words

per month, Johan   wet glass

of a particular unacceptable kind

   in earshot of

   Earth   an exit strategy

the recently-discovered skeleton

of a vice-umbrella

"on Honk Honk time"

              73 days of forced writing

              67 days of bargain whys

              34 days of industrial sorry

              764 days of lent

              360 days of vote sores

              8000 days of roach poses

              led
              by the conscience.

              Is it worth it

              the breast
              mightier than a head

A historical address
in an outrageous outfit

"rapidly approaching

§

the middle ages"

      O K
      I have needed a glass of water
      For a long time

excited by   long-term fatigue, and its strong performance

access to daylight was a big part of the work.

in theory   For a long time

Fantasy workplace:

"Think"
Does not occur.

I don't remember ordering this
Is the actual object, the global extension
The mango, the bike pump, the paywall
Swallowed by the language, or implicitly signalled
Although by this point
The language itself has become
General Chat Chat Lounge General Chat Chat Lounge

blue light
         green leaf

the detailed

patient

reassembly

of an entire

sensory life

rolling large stones across the landscape on giant felled trees
for the purposes of

moving   This morning

your ears.   Maple shade abundant.
                 Sidewalk gums.
I really do this,

                 Suddenly like yourself
I write   come in, take

                 a place

                        for

                     forgetting   *"fancy,"*
                                         a tree in
                  each other   *Pollok*
                                         park
                        together

                 in?)

                    the light changes, Jo
the pier swallows

last bit of paper

a distant
achoo

a song that hangs
in the air.

                  Esque-
esque.

A refrain on the bark
carved in the dark

it is good to be petty
about things that are pretty
yes it's 1986

watch it

upside down

blackbird sang

a doodle in the sand

of traffic pouring

Dear Oli

§

It's August, and I want a break from normal thoughts
In my usual design. It's July, and I put on a load of weight
For a long day of promises and worship
In the heat of the sun. But will my spells allow me to rest?
No, it was evening, and long months and endless happiness await us
In the house of childhood. We go there
By virtue of the people created for us:
L—, S—, D—, S—, S—, C—, G—, J—.
I gratefully acknowledge the effects of proper names
In anchoring me to a specific historical moment, an aesthetic tradition
Confused by my misuse. It's Thursday: should I sing
The green ground and the dark blue sky, the suspension
Of time in the occupied room, the steep crevasse, the casino
We failed to drink through. For a long time
We just wanted a baby. Now only one thing exists:
A thin layer of dust, a precipitate of a collision
The day forgetfully re-enacts as hard, unnecessary energy.
I'm always rushing to it—my nose almost hit
the horizon . . .
                    This is the low-point at which I realised
I should abandon familiar associations and turn to my subject,
The painting by Nicole Eisenman
Which gives this poem its title. I saw it in New York, in 2016, at the New
Museum, on a July day. There must have been some preparation,
Inadvertent or deliberate, a prior state of necessary dullness from which the act
Of looking at this painting represented a kind of escape hatch, or chute, out of
Or into the present. The painting offered an escape, maybe since it is partly
About escape, from itself and from the central figure, nearly asleep
At her designs, around which the other elements circulate
Almost reluctantly? I was going to go on with this
But I have nearly reached the end of the stanza. I will be back soon . . .

To leave and to return establishes trust, according to my book
About children. I am drawn to writings from the late nineteenth century,

Where I situate myself emotionally . . . but before I get to work on
     establishing my soul
Can I not? I remain drawn to the green earth
And the dark blue sky, yet the enduring, reactionary dream of stopping time
I was denied. This denial should also be the place to explain it,
This desire to place all my teeth beneath the pillow
But I'm already getting ready for the products and judgements that are
     part of the package
And even that scares me. The immense silence of the golf course.
I find all of this information so confusing I have to finish by accident and
     look back
At my theme, the picture by Nicole Eisenman
Which gives this poem its title. I first did this in 2014. In the first account
The viewer is depicted as a sort of witch, roach or rat.
The figure passes down the escape slide, for it is an escape from the self
And so on. The reaction is minuscule enough
That the recall's good enough to go on with, since now it is later, and
     everything has changed,
The morning has extended its hand and things have turned out alright
But also—not. A mild 11 o'clock in late April.
A short nap, but a good one

§

          doesn't quite work does it
          call it a cheville

          "what isn't inked
          isn't naked"

          now chill

§

Does feel weird to be tired
of a dream
in a dream

       of a happy
happy dream. How are
you.
Tired, happy, anxious

every open pore

the day that blisters

where it rubs.

Late afternoon light
like resurgent interest
italicising the tenements.

No planes.
More dads.
More pap.
What, tho

to sing
the sting
in listening

to rain
dehiscing

the lordly
briefing—

to want so
so little

to know
it's painful—

what—more
of that obvious

odour, more
that noxious juice?

before it cloy
like why

do you
dot dot dot

do that
out loud?

§

From one perspective,
        then, the work has relied
                heavily on vignette

based methodologies
        (e.g. luck, effort)
                to alter zygomatic

electromyographic
        activity. For example
                Johannes's office is about

fifteen long strides
        from the erotic court poetry
                found in Chapter 6

of the Declaration of Helsinki.
        (The function of uncertainty-bearing
                in an "imaginary figure" such as

Johannes is a "methodological
        makeshift.") As a child, I knew
                nine Juans. Another era.

I feel a lot of this
        as if one expects to feel
                this expectation may in fact

create its own reality.
        For example,
                participants who were shown

a picture of a world-class
        baby pointed straight at you
                and attempting to kiss

you passionately
        followed by a desert
                which has been punched in the face

causing one side to bulge out horribly
        were discouraged. Wait—he
                concludes his piece with a plea . . .

I totally agree with this conclusion.

§

Thankfully nobody remembers
what is meant by "that"

remember how you forget's
more interesting
than how you remember

what day, what name,
what song, what what

expressive, guessive.

Spend 3 mins
            whistling
through the lid
            of a biro.
Never get
            them back . . .

§

But
what to paste next
in this dumpy poem:

Sarah Vaughan's
            hum, minty
the tree stump,
            a picture
in which I
            awkwardly
prose, puns, hymns,

burns in the
paper so
    as to sug
gest a map,
    "a trap for
attention".
    Attention:

to bring together
things that long
to belong together

Lafarge   "a feeling of oblong"

Days pass . . .

the turning light spells
out trees, and birds, and the cars
phonetically

two new white hairs in my moustache

staggered deductions

it is possible to have a favourite
everything

just out of reach

kicked over a coffee
and remembered

the shadow a maple
made in April

unsure of the light source
deleting myself to death

I adhere to the lattice
like a locust

§

IP: 31.81.239.234
Timestamp: 2019-11-28 11:
11:30 UTC

I don't remember where I

woke up reaching for

the concentrate, the mystery tin

preserving the alternatives

Watching people go by

longingly or indifferently

from a distance of eight inches, it is this

to hold the iPhone up in the dark

to listen to the disappointing album

an almost physically painful task

"the station aflame"

I felt my interest returning, and yet

he really do this, he writes

listen, he draws

flicking the mesh, producing

a mixture of tiny brown, black, white and beige dots

first plane in months

pulsing in the garment

no argument

there you go

Wednesday, Thursday, Friday

remote

mote

§

To be in Cochabamba.

To be a girl again
snuffling
Adam's ketamine,

hallucinating gloomily in the garden.

For the face to be in the basin.

To be sick intensely in a hardly hedge

in a long, light dream.

"Sequester":

request
that we be
sequins

glinting privately
in the raiments
of May.

Written on pages
exported to word.

That ruse rouses us, true,
momentarily, as, under rain
thunder invents a radius

between refrains,
a spick span
to draw our listening

out
in.

Come in, late

say it with me, sweet

and easily: peg Dom

to a helium bunch

float him hastily

through the galaxy

brain towards the perfumed

hyperhusk that marks

our periphery. There,

meet Ronnie Corbett

in orbit. Just happy

to live in that

radiant playdate. The

abrupt vacuum

§

of coming. There

the clear Welsh river I unhear

bunches to a circumflex.

It's only after what feels like

never I notice how fucked

up the metrics are. The index

forgets

    I forget

which

    direction the arrow

should be pointing in.

Pointillism is invented in 2086.

Pop on your frock coat

and visor to visit truly

the worst genre. I'm afraid

I'll renege on my

promises to you, me,

torrenting said rain

from Nguyen.

But we've come this far
without meaning

to. Why start
now? Because

the novel's
a hovel

this poem
was built

as a lean-to
against. It

has a skillion roof
you can imagine

to summon snow
with, to bring

into being
the field

of statistics.
The children wave

to the bears
in the windows

with real sticks.
I visualise a sinkhole

in the shape of a swastika.
To pass the time

lie face down on a bed
of pins. And because there's

nothing quite like seeing a unique
3D impression of your face, love.

And for a month we did become
again a youngish couple.

We fucked ourselves the other with each.
Plain to chew with the jaw.

"Fathom": which
way round does
the metaphor go?

Yes, no, I don't know.

Something comes out in the language.
There's something here

I don't know.

4:50am: Out the bedroom window: entire sky of thin white
and grey cloud, moving slowly and all at once in one direction
(to my left) as if a vast net were being hauled in—though
there is under this uniform movement of cloud one clueless,
bulging, stationary outlier which hangs there as if observing
or omitted: flicker of sympathy into envy into happiness surge
at obligation and conditioning: I look at it, surcharged with
white (any intensification of colour reads as embarrassment)
with the pressure of knowing Ned and Frank will be up soon to
fill my attention's hole: a moment to think the word "Siberia",
to mouth it inside, infinite synonym, to think of a visit to Bath,
possibly, on a school trip, parts of a building (floors, walls) visible
beneath glass, a subterranean heating system involving steam
and bricks and tiles in little stacks layered like a Viennetta, then
the rich thicket of the music the mosaic makes

these things are
strung together—

we are "with"
each other

  when I ask
  you to count

your fingers
each morning

  the number
  changes, the

numbers
change.

Ned says dad
  you are mum
Frank is dad
  I am the
baby now
  you are the
baby I
  am mum Frank
is baby
  I wish I
had three dads
  two to work
and one to
  watch movies
with me no
  two to watch

and one to work
      where am I
dad your work
      is very
boring we
      are with each
other

(A few weeks to decide
how to break this line.)

Middle of June: endless day

A way of leaving

It all out

There.

This desire to expunge experience, or to pattern it in every
blob of putty.

A glassy—by which I mean see-through—pain. By which I
mean

A recurring dream: hundreds of mobiles of different colours,
ages, and sizes, dangling vertically from ceiling and floor. No
wind, but they move

POSTPOSITIVITY IN SPRING

1

So much
for poetry

and no
more. Perpetual

norm dawn
raising its awning

in purple
pose

for traffic
to battle

under galore. It's nice
to imagine you

sitting down
to write me

and putting it off.
Not to owe

is good but
to owe and be let

off is better.
Is that true,

sweetie? Or shall
I just

talk over myself
like rain

over
night

when the soft
ware up

date tunes
me up to spit

out wall to
wall wind

socks "come
morn." It's cool

in the shade,
warm in the

collapse
of the

avant sun
franchise

radiating out
across the retooled day

where nobody's
allowed in and

none of these objects
(the traffic, etc.)

are real, and
mean it.

2

Face up to it
enjambment

is not going
to sort your

face out. "Those
were difficult

days." That
browser

is no longer
supported

but you know
that. The

policy may be
that the screen

you're writing on
is not the screen

you're
reading.

It goes something like
the statement

of fact connects
us to a pin

and the pin refuses
to refuse and

in fact spreads
out everywhere

as a knowledge
slick. How

else can it be put
down. It's like

there is
no space

to which
to go

which is
a property

of space
to aggressively annotate, even

out here
where it becomes

untrue as
either urge,

to love
or not, becomes untrue

when pressed
hard enough

against
yourself,

like waves
flattened against

an upright
pane of glass

planted in
the middle

of the "flood
of subject."

3

There's a group
of isolated

new words like incoming
to step

up on
when the

desire to anything
is gone. This is

the uninhabitable
place after

becomes
now is

the final line
of this poem,

and then
the last

but now
how many,

ah ha. Funny
does it hurt less

it starts
to hurt

less.

LIVING, ETC.

1

Luke Luck flocks back to the joke tent or perhaps palace

pacing the loud loneliness, suddenly intimate,

intricate with internal noise . . .

clerihew cares . . .

2

Auguary, Septembuary, Octobuary.

Pure forlorn
sand dune porn.

I have like four lackadaisical friends
Louis and the beeboss
so mean and minor and still
Hufflepuff? Fuck off

"if we're ourselves
        a 401 to feed on"

"make music more
        than any song"

them's the
        books; very lit

to put in quote
as if written
in society

Very crowded. Guide is not interested
in his job

the yelp app
yelps deep down
in the Alps

3

One trillion one hundred fifty-one billion
two hundred seventy-two million one
hundred twelve thousand seven hundred fifty-
seven milliseconds in and still stuck out

in the interstices of the piece
turning to interning in
own life, plagiarising at 35
intimate, anonymous feeling

of feeling out for each other
by number, by torpor
working hard in the talk mine
working soft in the core pallor

back-combing archival grammar
to find one microscopic tick
and lock whatever
perverse personal novelty out

only to be logged immediately
back in

to the quarry room's
oculus for

one
last

excruciating bluetooth
mishap:

come, I entreat you, for
the nineties white rap

come
back

for the snowpuck
in discarded jockstrap

refreshing and refreshing
the Cabot

bot account,
whacking the trusty tin cup

to bring here to there, there
there, aware

of all our sounds inside
each other whenever

the cute moon races
above the glittery snowrock

inside the poem
reading body

every semi
surprising

hardcore
epoch

and for
what

saddo
glissando

that now you
are up to

my
taboo

corbeil
in far too

pain and
common

anexactly,
if not this?

4

Familiar collage
of foliage

fills in
the gaps,

jostles space
among your

tantrum's
upbeat.

Who doesn't
prefer bad art

to bond
over,

my dudes?
If only

for the sensation
of starting out

from wtf
and arriving

by
pain

staking in
advertent

disassembly
note by

phone
me at a common

weakness: shy
greys and vague

blues: raggedier
tea towel

blots
of white

coming up hard:
inauspicious

morning
from

which intimation
can be set

in motion
again

5

Some kind of
frantic music

has just started
up outside

and it's bad news if you're a Carolyn, Debra
Greg or Walt

pausing before the giant Cambridge teapot . . .
wait am i ded

Violet, Meryl, I'm thinking now of what you said
my sink, my place of work

begins since
socks I have no day

and night and night and night and day
and only on the lightest weights

I work me out
to how to say

please go to sleep, please go
in and don't

come out until
I work out how

to say
this out. I email these lines to Sam

and he replies
lol no

6

Here I lye Clock a clay

a billion oclock on a February day

bad actors hijacking good research

bad actors selling pruning shears

Voice security issues. All ears

Ok, good, again, fine
to be held to what isn't mine

these mysterious objects, residual tech
shining among the myrtle leaves

noun noun
noun noun

Who's looking after them
while you're doing your
shirk wrong?

Pick up epic
put it down

erratically balanced on
a balancing rock.

I actually like the deepfaked head
in that squishy urn over here

suspiciously listening back.
Listening back suspiciously

to this note
over where exactly

I shush and click my fingers
click and shush at you, sill bird

7

Art, brainless Art!

Leisure is pain. You heard

DINGDINGDINGGEDICHT

Yes to panic;
Cool projective pragmatism, one hundo

Unbitted sexual life—
17th century wheat revival: mammal glow

{Zealand}

Yeah—yes. Feels good

Evil, watching the dream
Game spaced in prospect
Everything's possible, nowt

Sad not to know how it concludes
Relieved, disinterested
Even my own cruelty
As it blurred your face this morning

Cigarette out on wet wall, personal detail
Contracting sharply within the rim of it, which is what?

Regret showing you the shit bit
So soon, suffice to face
The snow melts loudly
Soaking through my right shoe

I want to put the snowroom inside me.
But you can't let your guard down around that guy. What guy.

It's then I get this twitching in my
Whatever this twitching's for? To serve
And surveil, with ambassadorial mildness
The skip fire, the quasi-adjectival future
Like some roaming orbicular gourd (hehe god??)

Amazing paper on the tree
Of heaven is a weed btw. By "you"
I mean pronominal parapraxis
Familiar from earlier in the fire rite

Glistening soft joist
Moistening your ellipsis
Gross, horny

Imitating what's around you
Bringing it in, disgorging it
Forgiving it its distinctiveness

In the privacy
Of absolute openness
Inside the poem, for the curiosity
Of infinity friends, laying it out in error
On institutionally headed paper
On the rainbow summer hosepipe spray
The apple harvest, the zombie meme, not only
To clyppe, to stretche, to adde, or chaunge
Or in fact foorget weyre the citation's frome

Zoned out a bit there, fantasising bourgeoisly
Which brings me back to the proposed theme
The collective disturbance in our dreams
After the great storms of 1703 and 1987.
These were turning points

But the angles of the turn were acute
Rather than obtuse, I think, and what with the way
I still don't know you. I mean shut my mouth
But that still seems like a kind of chance.

EARTH FROM

The murmur
of an um
and an

er, etc.,
sustains the
"apparent present"

through "stains
in the day"—
whatever

precedes us
seeds how
we guess

I guess.
Little bits
of anguish

showing you
how to
distinguish

foot from
earth from
star from

song to
chew off
and on.

WANTING ANOTHER

1

Float and fret
air, rain; intricate rain air;
sonnetness of the autumn
flowers ouch OK.
I guess that's much
closer to, left of
early daylight
chintzing the sea,
the attempt not to be
affected by it while
writing it, super-position
scooping out
what shows,
which shows.

2

    giant
        gnat

      heaven
              on ear
    even on
        floor

hundreds of people on the beach
        waiting blue sea
              smell of the white
          inside orange
            peel inside
               the journal or

shit tore

fireworks starting to go off 5000 miles away, threatening wakings

3

anxiety is only another
kind of movement
in many directions
at once, slightly many

looking out of window over misty valley
at dusk, murmuring, "Renault . . ."

4

the gulf

moon rises

its flag

over the bay;

a car alarm

goes off

and on

bufferingly

EARTH IV

A sweet retreat from the responsibility
Of being a person, separate
From sensation's confetti, life
Fluttering on the screengrab surface?

The private vanities of vanishing points
Each friend and statement
Has a shape nice or ugly—
E.g. David, plus David's gravity

Six o'clock shadowing
Like a Pepsi Max hiss
Greying in just now the diagram
Of your avoidance of certain facts

About your life, involving a life
You have been falling into
And out of while pausing. I hardly
Feel it then only softly do.

SLEEPERS AWAKE

It's the Yoker sky fragments
or the perma-yellow

period pollutants in the brushwork
you can't slate for. It's

the child crooner
approaching, demanding your day

even while it's snowing.
It's starting to skip

conceding the words
are in place, the familiar refrain

ruined by the potency
of the awkward echo,

the pareidoliata in a visible
voicenote. It's what I do

each morning, along Argyle Street
the era's method, hidden

in plain daylight's
copyrightlessness

reduced to a grain
of an origin

yet to happen. It's those
skinny tree

shadows again
webbing the park rink

like a cracked plate, basic
whitecold day, slyly

over a thousand others
overpromoted. It's your eyes,

the phone you do. Is it sickness
knocking me on the basics

it's snowing again. It's snowing
heavily all over Glasgow

making everything naked
and light, a face

relaxed at last. At first it's
snuffed day sound echoes

that you too
only have to hear about distantly

to not know how it feels
when you move always

from room to day to
early dusk, forced

by forgetting, thinking, Siri
what even was I about to ask

what's wrong? It's the no ice
in noticing I sing, puff puff,

the airy you-form of January
without rigour or shame

in gorgeous rouge sun,
renting its blush

from the sandstone
deepening into dusk

as if embarrassed, but pleased,
to be perceived. I

wanted all of that, for
myself and you, buggy

squeak, tight air, Kelvin
slush and easily more

from which a gaping
ear may nosh

on a bad day, blandness
in serial form. Fat clouds

over Campsie Fells in slo-
mosh. Flat clouds, cowhides,

an association I semidesigned
and love for that

designed-feeling,
its failure, impermanence.

Later bits of snow slowly
clearing themselves

on the window, dittoing
the dark day, they were there,

here. Glad to have
sung it for you once.

NOT LEY LINES

Wintry
twigs make
a pernickety
clicking sound
among blotches of January
window light, post-panic white . . .

*

Cooling hot milk
in an ice bath
today's screaming.
Roaming the ratios
like a diorama
rubbernecking vernacular
I basically don't what it

*

Leave the
dishes to

look up
a theory

word on
my phone

hold the
big noun

in my
other hand

up down
squinting, ishing

exposure sloshing
in side

and parts
to repeal

in instalments
ash dab

on my there
fore head

*

Still frilling around objects with a Jacobean
ruff. Freaked out, set a tea towel on fire . . .
Your poem says put that in one of your poems
for drunk relief, to frolic in leaf
so familiar now I hear it before it happens
a kind of hologram, a blotchy aura
of fungibility, written down January 33rd
orthogonal to the line, the "sun's lesion"
in the curved upside time of the poem's
akin to being rude to a spoon. Just listen to
this tune, embarrassinging our room . . .

THEORY OF THE LYRIC

The ich bin.
The ick bucket.

The ice palace
plug socket.

Now we're talking.
Come here—please.

OK, everyone.
Go back to York.

This one's for Rick.
This one's for

everyone who's
ever done it.

But what is "it"?
An instrument?

Happy birthday
Rick. Not guilty.

Toke the mic.
Kick it. Fuck it

HENOHENOMOHEJI

My face is blue, his fingers are disappointing, OK.
Until you comb yourself, looking for fruit dots
where it feels so sweet, so tightly woven, kicking up dust
as it's rummaged. Like it's time to feel something inside
the moment, which is obviously not there in some sense,
when the world sculpts a little around you, even though you are everyone
and all the mixed and exaggerated light blips and twigs outside
the feelings inside, which pour out as a blush . . .

The panic of openness towards chance, and the necessary period of
    desperation that follows
such as she does not want to go to school, and says no, I don't want to.
Images are not allowed, except for blizzards and rockets, fleshing
the intensity I didn't yet know was a weak reflex.
I'm reading this instead of whacking my head for example
in the direction of the pain, or is it joy, that all this already existed.
There are creatures who feel that their trouble is rooted somewhere under
    the fees.
Then the prism of Spring, pulling blossoms from its branchsleeves . . .
Eating the noun nearer.

BUTTERY WHATABOUTERY

This shyness deep down's about nibbling
that honking's about the post

8.37 sunrise:
shambolic redpink

wincing with Andrei, pausing
choux-delicately between past and oral

between Milngavie voiced, unvoiced, wincing
that the monograph was fire emoji

that the sounds
the words make

the words the
sounds make

with each other . . .
solidarity . . . curly whiskers . . .

those clouds, tho
incred

Dropping down into a deep round role.
Eating these beans with your tongues. But beans
aren't snail horns; and snail horns aren't
tongues. OK, so? No, that oak tree's not
a trochee. Watering the basil
pot not just with tears, but with Oscar
snot. The hourly transfiguration
of our lovely sun-eating. A head
segment that's now a broodsac; now a
mouldy glasshouse orange. Delivering
these thoughts to October and to crotch.
Saturdays throughout the war, cranking
in a frenzy . . . Calling time upon
moribund gerunds, parasitic
noise, yes-nose. So much for Nottingham.

THE OPERA BUFFA BUFF, BIFF, SOUNDED DEAD

Getting the shared towel sopping wet
like the bar magician, Ian. See how

technical language has its own pickpocketable beauty
like residential permit, like mesenteric adenitis, like me googling

at your thoughts in the night
with my always-on transferable litigious headtorch

blackening the Catullus rampart
at night, intestinal Biennial night

Baby beached asleep and wondering
if after so many you wonder as I sometimes do

however sweetly, Ian,
but now what are you up to?

LOVE HACK

Dark search . . . has life not secretly faded
with the increased clarity of the night, though we remain
bitterly out of normal work?? It was like this on Tuesday
clicking away, the head crackling away
how, I notice, when an hand is at its most curious
the curiosity, as it goes on, extends its narrowness to the medium, unique
    pseudo-growth . . .
It's embarrassing that there is so much of it and that he talks exactly the
    way he can
but there's also a kind of richness and resound.
The conscience is electrified and immediately discarded, something

eyes stick out at like a bad line. Sure
I pump the concrete out and I'm a paddle, and sure I'll tape myself
not knowing any better; my guess is, yes,
it was erected as an unfortunate but necessary force, this Chamber of
    Ignorance
which makes me especially vigilant, so much so that up to the present
    hour
you continuously refer to me as a deadly baby, who cannot know even
if I do not know. A block dump of thousands of years of information
gawps the air-water, waves like it's missing us already.

MAY FACE

This fact of maximum resistance
looking into people's houses in the evening, early summer
the steeply receding strata of the rooms which have factored us in already
though unaware, out in the mesh of analytical errata
except as a gnome Q-team listlessly
plugging in and out of public sockets: suck it up
the cold force of certain tags, cabinets, pets, melodies
or suck it up, the Clyde turning turtle
in its inlet, in blue and pink and brown turning
pink and brown and blue.

ON NOT BEING ABLE TO WRITE

One stalled a voice
to steal a second with

       wait
           thwart

the "ailment of close
alignment"

       gorgeous

ness of mess
made by our head

caves. Corn flake
plankton swirl
broke piano
slick duck

sound the real thing

gong. Perma-March
merch outside
        wet
     blossoms

black tile tenement
       roof, four
floors up in the poem

and you a real
                ghoul in the room
                is what I heard
pulling the algomelody
every which
                day. Maybe
anything
seems

more alive with what's
                        not

said, reptile origins
        of. At the friendship

                        shop, at archive
park, at sea loch men

suspended in albumen
don't seem alive
                about it
whatever grows
        slower

than a smallpressed flower
        forms. For a while
I wanted you
        more than me.
        A lonely coterie
                eye
            volleyed back

lists, tenses, trustfalls, trifurcations
plenty thorny wattage.

Indexed
        together the way
we'd disagreed:

Roof, flower, plankton,
piano, neptune, zinc, cum . . .

coming back again to flytip our shit
wonkily on the landscape

not changing it slightly
completely.

COMPOSED AT ERDBERG

I

Going forwards
into zinc motes
buggily humming

a maything song
I almost lurch
to punch my own

voice, crushingly
loud in airpods
cancelling the moor

of shuffled spruce,
rushes, and larch.
Before I or

anyone knows
a yelp comes from
our inbox out

II

What if the "way" of melancholy
is via a fiddly melody
the basic idea of which
is dead; she understands
through melody
the basic idea that

you die; or the method
of melancholia
is an awkward song
from which one basic idea
has expired; if self-denunciation's
juggling hexagonal
piano patterns back to
yourself in agog air,
too ornamental
to be severe. Apostrophes
as the poem starts to snow
itself, as though—"apostrophes
like snow begins to fall
on poetry"—succumbing
to the environment,
giving in to it, since to clock
something partial's
the payoff for being
a person short of
a person, the existential
reward of being a short man
alone. Because it's a tense thing,
not nothing, to feel about
the freshness of the feel
of HD spruce leaf.

III

Probably time
to doodle

up a
song you

can look
at or

not. The pieces
do not

have tempo
indications

and recordings have ranged
from under 2 minutes

to over 4 minutes
in length for all six.

IV

Scratching
something irrational

on noise, that is
scratching when

you scratch
with noise, that is:

scratching while scratching
something useless

with useless
sound.

V

Not a waste
to waste
the fluorescing

misreading
reach of a
wren's wrung

routine.
Until the shine
comes on

it is misread
as access to the
Mutilated Warbler

one regular, disgusting
evening.
Jay called again

about the cosmetics.
Despite his
sweetness,

he leaves
a feeling
in you.

VI

Sorting recycling in
Eden—when

in doubt
shout—

the boxy rumble
of one consoling form

of indecision
verberating

through June . . .
Brush brush.

Playing it again
in the bland toy landscape

when in
doubt.

Literally just knocking
about with you

in the and
of the

inging
room.

NOT YET

...no I don't
know how to
defend the present
tense or to
finish or to
not appall these
great travails so
gladly spent (Sir
Thomas Wyatt, "Forget
not Yet the
Tried Intent") except
to go back
down to the
beginning again and
fall its parts
up through the
poem in slow
motion, at once
cautious, and also
kind of curious,
as in a
very far down
brown puddle a
single speck of
white and purple
streetlight is "hammered
in to clouds"...

I

Now shall I continue telling about the growth of finger memory as is my preference
or be live-dated by a recent day of memory placement that this person
(meaning "individual head blockage") moved from such a conversation (which I,
a person, spend fearing) to finding why finding the term "memorable" was the joke

as with the interior, the social time indicator, the face like good parents I knew
daydreaming for us constantly an employer, a substance somewhere
goodnight nature world, the existence hymn of enough watching machinery
its language will part purposefully, gently part or even end up partly hoping

for visible place spots, blotting as cloud-cover the encounter which eases
public re-enactment and is still towing about for a punch in the middle–soul
or even panic in pleasure, even if what pleasures anyone is to be an absolute
face which inward-turned calls forth, mother-more-unique, such a face

who expressionless to this maquette is drawn, then, as location, as place-
name, since each object kind object has purposelessness, an air of only on-air
impossible wildlife, since it could pencil whole an installation of the time
before this moment and I still wouldn't know how to find you

=

To advance this letter then I developed a fear of even qualifying for morning
and outside temporary opposition everywhere is peak actual just songs I quote
another dream world, but hand I'm censure, the football-haunted pronoun
and it is our feet, our burrowing scepticism, pulsing in the speaking

room with like people and group consequence, hallucinating why the work
in failure would never continue to would, since opinions, but with whips
the even matter was parted, taken down, on and on, the checking course
on which we have gone, the distance, their holding—what—and its story

like external footage blended, exaggerated and one, preferably mother
feels around the interior, our actions as turns, things, and even conditions
does my object blue his fingers, that disappointment, fine long like suddenly yourself
brushed you, and through the unhappy compromise if u text me

winning moments of art, the white responding it could make me itself
caught an itch which, one awful, struggling episode, stretched beyond 5pm
very what's accepted, very safely braided ago, the dusty hope when equivocating
is to feel something to a present not at extent, where the world shelves the tiny you

Nature is my office, then, fill the blush in, see how Rousseau punches
a nation-state sculpture sense of reading this about the punch coming more
sweetly in time, teach it, mother, turn it through some whoever velvet,
that moment (which, from central expertise, a window "supposedly immediately

opens on"), remembering the July anecdote as the tough bit now of nearby sadness
that spikes an experience into you, and might even make a serious friend of it—
a light mood yet hardly lavish—so to have contrived something
I was certain I found up to confirm the embarrassment of an injury painted on

borrowed panic which was darkness registered or simply made giant by drinking
the openness of which, against woods and sense-period placed,
permits no pics but of clauses spreading, a fictive grey,
a severity I didn't know as my own, poor reflective thing

and yet sitting double leader of my incapable section, forensically mounting
the hidden sky, become from the forty-minute mark standard disclosure
to finally giving in at a story of unusual being which so repels, even I,
considering the mood of it, struggled then to get up and say

IV

For there were lived minutes and apparent rooms, existed out genuinely
at which my decision or that as a child, a holding to account, or film of how life is
a memory when it's asleep, images I lens detectably confirming perhaps
the struggle of reading when cut thinking it, terminology rendered as if of work

one feels the pain, since really largely necessary like the utopian Lord airport
whose misfortune I feel answers roots somewhere many assemblies down
this being, not the small pain of it, just up and evaporated on the basic air
as if wonder is by environment, thorn and sleeve, its book sense extended

the particular Henry ribbon corner song of wandering away
that's really about the leave feeling, such as yes you may dress the absolute worst
but nor could our technological couple who hum the centre to keep
intimacy placidly smiling as the thing, the little strangeness

replacing the wince explanation like the actual maybe of couple think
as explanation about keeping the sentence meat clear
while our son levels
us with the new-found thirty thinking (while you cry)

v

And after actually recalling when desire had left a suspect vent
such powerless accuracy, feel, suppose, what the love idea is sometimes
the exhaustive insurance with phantom leads, as of wonder, of which
the discomfort, unexpectedly—and I among material over-appeared,

a slowly perceived outfit trying the best copy-and-paste general joy
which powers pragmatically past to an original felt in ourselves, a reproduction,
dark retrieval, someone to explain living never gone though, secretly or felt
in summer, cumulatively, your presence, stranger sequence, actual present night

holding referendum time, still when substantially, remember, elaborating
hard memories of shopping, completely, for a single-syllable atmosphere
and all it ended up was being of dreams, the picture becomes a boring time thing
an overly eccentric evening, with night incrementally perceptible

around the sky's heels, says key feeling of luminous melting
because my touching there's meaning I gratefully experience life,
phenomenon of a guess portal as deep surface only with whispering—
minor day crimes, yes, but friends, Tuesday has a time foothold

VI

So since I text Caboto and pretend you'd rate me as a sensual world
he dropped a pin on Neptune, the centre cell
upskilling the interior into obtrusively confessing to having prepped a cool soliloquy
an eleventh free fiction of an animating European hesitation among pyramids

first introduction to deterioration modulated to taking Amanda's memory
of a retreat from an OK job in a hard-feeling way (it's been such a Monday
that the footage, the lives, during which the clearly different on camera
are at eye-level aware of being conscious of having felt violated, have been coming to

or *at* me when it's dark, changed, as someone I know only by the flicker of exposure
of their intent to sense via annual semifrantic holiday hate agony escalations
—not that through which a still moral is streaked consistently—becomes
suddenly invested in growing my soul, lengthy excursions on the PlayStation,

why flaws in football's self-consciousness—the authoritative "somehow" of it—
mapped itself pristinely as I would be, laying bare a system of reluctance
to the going harmony, the e-fitness, the contrafactum of the it
turning beautiful at last, the consequence of which is where we begin

113

VII

Yet in the interest of performance April kept flouting scene convention
a distant tapping, the cancelled promontory seen moving content secretly back into space
like disgust banging out golden shapes just off page, yet smiling was still my thing,
the rhomboid strikes as exact as somedays someone says sure Catholicism

or I should've been a space achilles, and the solid earner is to want completely
my us, our me, all lives wanted alive for plants are merely for magic-eye
since won't is now in my would skiff, then just suppose with yr million position hat on
the smaller me as a trope of detection, light crackling from the rhythm in misunderstanding

like, I note, when an hand seems to be saying something possibly most tainted
in unusual metres it becomes signatory of a permanent shape
surfaces present as internal owing to
their appearance as a series of lines we face patterned up the playground wall

like have fuck, can order, will nail walking my time backwards through the changed book
world, since you're duration, a stretch for the internet, unique false overgrowth
of the eye having brunch in the sketchiest west hand embarrassed wife creation
who cannot get this synonymous, cannot shake it: sexy plant consciousness

VIII

Thousands of slightly altered Williams whipped it like that
where writing sounds its distance, schools time
the general after-ache of etymology boomering down the mysteriously postponed
explanation of pleasure in polite recognition of my clearly actually changing

and you, across a vast room
seem like a fresh opportunity to fail to write,
to spill the song
embarrassingly, which with that much more and talking exactly he might

earn as pleasure, like learning in the direction of another speed to Latin
allowing through the redwood, touching an equilibrium of story dots
(it is partly my non-feeling for visible things controlling me, leaves me vaguely striving
in my bedroom, imagining how R's trouble guides the darker passages

or getting pristine through self-obliviousness), further extracted couple ruptures
deflate the concrete and I racket I'd ribbon out through the work window
having no Spanish one night I put forward a motion to self to "get to Cairo"
so said alcove, so celestial suburb, so skin in which I've contrived to semi-live

IX

Ten further uncertainties go ahead sighing at the infrastructure
turning meat into cloud so I had something to think this morning
still I weather the designed feeling, proceed to recommend my leg
extends North so that I may begin retracting it by Christmas—as our 2013 specialist

of the unable torso in middle-age I'm the first to feel intensely lucky
to touch Rousseau's commercial person, yet my conversation
including the larger realm of daydream directly tells me of winning wires of guilt
taped alive throughout the memory card, forever—out of such shape-shifting

widened draining moments of intensest self-alarm are cleared a bunch of sockets
to seem annoyed we're at the Olympics in, where my most hollow-seeming versions
seem suddenly very persuasive to one another, dramatised figments
of whatever knowledge remains happy-disastrously unavailable

on the subject of these meagre feelings, and as deferentially I'm then to mean anything to anyone
can that problem think me there, present on a criticism hill—
if all were peculiar, a promotional dream-world, and accurately
notional, yes, a pitching keyboard is exact work (which existing causes)

X

Crab lab hack, meet familiar world man
triggering objects, advertising a moon
erected as unhappy authority projected towards background night space
overtaken by the fictionalise department, a present frozen

by a crayon on the air, thank u, ash stub, surprising with some new expressive pattern
angling for response from your organ-tree, touched, only lightly, line-by-line,
with a set of striking passwords—input and unexpectedly forgot—lacing the hours
with potent feelings of self-worth about capacity to master the room tone syllabus

dropping a naturalness crisis surge, until I would find myself asking
would I be surprised to be too embedded in this documentary
state to recognise my own lie, to put that German suit on to bask
in the vivid logic of the solar block broken by the barn yarn

to conclude a thin childhood recalled on horseback
via a superimposed diagram—the folkloric
slow hallucination of the light, maybe my parents
specifically arming me to be at the enormously crucial detail suddenly quite alert

The terrible thing is to have made of him a book—or to have pressed undeterred
though a room of non-knowledge always there yet mostly presumed to be "off"
towards an unhelpful clock directed at it, "the whole"—only to experience
stage two of this environment, environment Z, too abruptly, the insertion

of which phenomena in my daydream slog instantly normalises everything
and leaves only faintly especially ourselves, a "skim-read" sensation finding its antonym
as cast-iron daylight toggling its doubt finger, crowning art as the major hobby era
as though warmth for others were simply a doubling of obtuseness, a television

I attack with a fork (time to admit, Rousseau, the form my defence of Things
took: the redwood was about to mulligan it)
like a failed interviewee, meaning in the life hour I sit alone drawing
in the culture of morning light, my jacket releasing previously closed-off

art whispers and dimensions, here, mastering my experiencing style,
the clauses of feelings fresh and familiar, and what else is there to detect in regard to their source
but functional generosity, an in-house hygienic horror, publications like
"my reason for doing things," 335 Modern proper thoughts

Inevitably I became extremely well-read in Renaissance screaming
and so translated: "Great path, I was recently promoted
to writing generation T, where Progress terminated Dance, and from my ledge looked back
at your staring wounds with the poise of a Sundial, taking in the old program

because my year timelines me into autofictional schedule 6 (fear of discrepancy)
with a shocked sense that my own, speak it, selfhood, had been solicited to tell
of some forty dreams of sick air responsible for a funded green fashion height feeling
of brittle happiness on a social hill which the flats around, displaying unflustered constituents

of resolution, of 10-minute truly meant ideas which imagine the heat of
a multimillennial infodump to hold, to be beheld, permitted me to be plugged into the someone
who, as all know, knows all about the importance of writing
at particular fortress locations, the general importance of safety writing

from the scene of the fact pipe on highways closing in on us,
as living blurs us, flimsier, makes us seem but that we live only careless lives
implied ever since by history, in so small a role the dots
used to denote them were as fanfic to the so-called longstanding theory of *unassailability*

XIII

The thousand-language chore of extracting stuff from forgetfulness
is my office, then, colour the essay in, let our head interiors
touch to position the spotlight on the increasingly fatalistic toddler
who argues powerfully through an off-key melody

for the jovial texture of batshit relations, for the pleasure
of live-drawing in sceptical company—sometimes I want to be overheard exhaustively
like a relaxed coward, cartoonish as a ribbon on a soliloquy wind, yet still well-thought-of
as though alert to the at-any-moment call for total interior re-enactment

as a series of disembodied caveats, loops of sunlight
doodled on the polished floor which moves everyone at the loop recall funeral
a response I like, but, mum, it seems time that thousands and a few things
Monday expressed by spilling such evidence of blackout non-seriousness

must follow me down the spilled SEO architecture
towards the fat, bottle-green moment of medieval Tokyo, shone and buffeted
by large wings of anger and nervousness
the shook spot, chequered with hesitation, where I stay

XIV

The day knew the course, slightly angling towards the moment
when I lower my eyes, and the abrupt blankness of 1000 things
(these explanations of how I am what I am and why)
vibrates with a mischievous intensity, as if knowing it's being looked at

untangles into a promise of simplicity
a tangle of simplicity which binds the environment you've built around you
averaging out the fabrications, the decent freedoms
the social concepts which harden like a diamond

when their permanence is questioned, a question formed under the massive pressures
of regrets shifting slightly violently over epochs
how I dream of you, anxious, in which your seemingly-infinite indifference
to my discomfort wounds like a live crime

delicately implied, a cryptic reference to this bearable skin, felt disaster
roaming in the hope of historical love on the good ship my face
literally a few lovely days, a consequence of murder,
where these people are quiet as they repeat their explanation

XV

To advance then this perverse investment in the skies' continuation
I fact-check the script, underline Irrawaddy for a leisure google
feel the jigsaw of the minute assemble itself
as a stomach panic complexes into a series of narrow moods

I will wave off laterally through the lukewarm night—vintage May
season of magnetic decision-making, of imagined holy fucking
as though desire were a spy fluid, an overly agreeable thing
badly translated from the unhappy, surging like a delayed joke

to electrify a pronoun and be immediately ostracised: something
the eyes cancel as bad font, recalled product of disorganised commercial thinking
that pulls you together into a direction, towards the hole where the mosaic turns,
homesick for loneliness—tossing parts in the tub

frightened to stay alive, the misdirections leave their own precipitate
a glittering campaign of counter-assumptions
surely a day for intimacy, for infraction
for hurt to feel common, unknown

XVI

But shall I continue telling about an actually inconsistent state
a "bubble" overrun with melochemical elaborations, not even a finger's depth
only baroque, childish balustrades, brusque examples of global pain
in memory uniform which become in delay combination a trick pleasure

a Germanic dream-world or provincial glass structure, lit from within
by the infinite ocean—a stage for innocuous, ethical days,
where happiness's a soundless calendar by which to trace the jargon
incurred by fluency this morning—that's the kink, decision's shingle

that I mid basic, asleep in pieces, slurried in the technical morning
felt as do-able, where I do the loving at you
in briskly decorated open dream secret
and yet I'm still only capable of laughing nervously, C, what is it

to be following in spiral a precise point as the basin drains
towards a blanket powerout in the iris of the Earth
a memory of a nice feeling motioning my hand in disbelief
to a point, a precise point towards which these objects now stream

§

ACKNOWLEDGEMENTS

Versions of some of these poems have been published in *Blackbox Manifold*, *Harper's Magazine*, *Ludd Gang*, *Poetry London*, *Poetry Review* and *Wyrm*. "Progress: Real and Imagined" was published as a pamphlet by SPAM Press in 2020. Many thanks to the editors.

I would like to acknowledge the support of the Leverhulme Trust, which provided me with a research fellowship to help with the writing of this book.

Thank you to those who helped these poems happen in one way or another: Lucy Hazzard, Denise Bonetti, Kirsty Dunlop, Sophie Collins, Hugh Foley, Dom Hale, Sam Harvey, Maria Sledmere, Honor Hamlet, Caleb Klaces, David Spittle, Ben Doller, Graham Foust, Adam Piette, Alex Houen, Mark Ford, Maureen McLane, Ben Lerner, Andy Ching, Parisa Yekalamlari, Fred Carter, Daisy Lafarge, Harriet Moore, Michael Schmidt, John McAuliffe, Andrew Latimer, Jazmine Linklater, Katie Liptak and Jonathan Galassi.